YELLOWSTONE
and the
GRAND TETONS

Featuring the photography of

Edmund Nagele F.R.P.S. & Eberhard Streichan

Designed and Produced by

Ted Smart & David Gibbon

MAYFLOWER BOOKS, NEW YORK CITY

IN his lifetime, John D. Rockefeller gave away more than $500 million, thousands of it a dime at a time, and almost no one ever said "no, thank you". But when his son, John D. Rockefeller, Jr., tried to give a gift of $1,500,000 to all the American people, he got involved in a battle that lasted 22 years and even included a Congressional investigation during which a Senate Committee earned itself a lot of newspaper headlines by looking the Rockefeller gift horse in the mouth.

The gift horse was more than 33,500 acres of land in a beautiful valley in Wyoming called Jackson Hole.

Rockefeller loved the place. "The Teton Mountains are, to my way of thinking, the grandest and most spectacular mountains I have ever seen," he said. "When viewed over the vast expanse of sagebrush which covers the valley, or with Jackson Lake and the marshes in the foreground, they present a picture of ever-changing beauty which is to me beyond compare."

His love affair began in the summer of 1926 when he took a vacation trip to Yellowstone National Park. Part of the red carpet welcome he was given was a tour guided by park superintendent Horace Albright. Three years before, Albright had met with a group of local people at Maud Noble's cabin at Menor's Ferry and together they devised a plan to extend Yellowstone Park south to include the Tetons. They proposed that the antelope and buffalo herds should be increased, and theorized that the money to do the job ought to be donated by wealthy men who had followed Teddy Roosevelt's lead and made this their private hunting ground. Albright had plenty of what's known today as "charisma", but not enough to shake that much money loose. Two years later, in 1925, 100 landowners drew up a petition offering to sell their land for recreational purposes because they were convinced it wasn't good for much else. No one seemed interested in that idea, either.

By the time Rockefeller arrived, a great many land-owners had taken the bull by the horns and built gas stations, erected billboards, opened motels. Some had just walked off the land, leaving abandoned buildings to rot. Albright showed Rockefeller the mess and told him about the plan developed at Miss Noble's cabin. Mr and Mrs Rockefeller "did not make any comments on the proposal," said Albright later. "Nor did I reiterate anything I had said, nor did I ask for their support. None of us mentioned the subject again."

Rockefeller did ask for a map of the area he had seen and told Albright to estimate the cost of buying the run-down properties. A few months later, Albright went to New York with a roll of maps under his arm and a cost estimate of $280,000. "You misunderstood," said Rocke-feller. "You showed me an ideal. I am only interested in ideal projects." What he had in mind was to buy the whole valley. And, although Albright estimated that would cost more than a million, the "ideal project" got underway in 1927 when the Snake River Land Company began quietly buying the Jackson Hole Valley.

And that was when the trouble began. Some years later, columnist Westbrook Pegler said the activities followed "the general lines of Adolph Hitler's seizure of Austria." Presidential hopeful Thomas E. Dewey blamed the New Deal for this "lack of responsibility for the rights and opinions of the people affected." But former President Herbet Hoover hailed it as "a great gift...one of the great recreational areas in the United States."

Small ranchers in the valley were pleased to sell. Long, hard winters made ranching unprofitable for them, and the Snake River Company was paying fair market value. But the bigger ranchers didn't want herds of elk on their grazing land. Local officials wondered where they'd get money to run their government if the county became Federal land. And to add fuel to the fire, the United States Forest Service, who controlled the mountains, wanted to keep control of timber in the valley and was determined to keep the National Park Service at arm's length a few miles north of Yellowstone. They lost the first round when Congress created Grand Teton National Park in 1929. But Jackson Hole was not included and the controversy surrounding it got so heated that the House Appropriations Committee cut off all but necessary maintenance funds for the park three years later.

The politicians and the conservationists fought it out until finally, at the end of 1949, President Truman signed a bill that put the Jackson Hole National Monument (a designation given to it by Presidential proclamation after the land was formally given to the Government in 1943) within the boundaries of the park. Through it all, Rockefeller never gave up on his "ideal project". But while the fighting was going on, he quietly donated $2 million to save California's redwoods, another $1.5 million to protect the Yosemite pine forests and $5 million to help establish Great Smoky Mountains National Park back east.

While he was at it, he built a park at the northern end of Manhattan Island, and after turning it over to the City of New York, turned around and bought a 13-mile stretch of the New Jersey Palisades, just to preserve the view.

But the Grand Teton project was the one he considered most important, and once the people accepted his gift, he went to work on a development program that involved building a whole village of 209 log cabins on the shore of Jackson Lake, a lodge and cabin complex on Jenny Lake, and a $6 million, 400-room hotel. When work began on the projects, the Park Service announced it would set the pattern for development in virtually all the National Parks, and the promise has since been kept.

Colter Bay Village, named for John Colter, who is credited with "discovering" Jackson Hole and the geysers of Yellowstone, includes log cabins that can sleep up to six persons. The biggest of them, which each have two rooms and a connecting bath, rent for $35-$50 a day. A one-room cabin, for one or two persons, costs under $20.

If you like to rough it, Colter Bay Village also has "tent cabins" which rent for under $15 a day. Each has a wood-burning stove and an outdoor grill. Inside are two double-decker bunks, a table and benches. Bedding isn't included, but sleeping bags, as well as cooking utensils and other gear, are available for rent.

The Grand Teton Mountain Range previous page *and viewed* above *from Snake River,* began as a gigantic fault block uplifted from the earth's crust. Sculptured by streams and glaciers, these spectacular peaks now form a chain of pyramids, soaring more than a mile above the sagebrush flats and morainal lakes of Jackson Hole.

The range's highest peak, Grand Teton *below left* and *below, and seen* left *from Snake River and* above *and* below right *from the Rockefeller Memorial Parkway,* rises to a breathtaking height of 13,747 feet above sea level.

Some of the glaciers which gave the range its present form still remain and frigid glacial lakes dot the landscape. Of these possibly the most famous is Jenny Lake which lies motionless at the foot of Grand Teton and Mount Teewinot overleaf.

Set among the Grand Teton Mountains, Jackson Lake below left, *shimmering at twilight* above left, *rose-tinted at dawn* overleaf *and burnished gold at sunset* left *and* right, *is a natural lake formed in a deep groove left by a piedmont glacier which passed through Jackson Hole during the first Ice Age.*

Flat-topped Mount Moran above, *still capped by a remnant of the old sea bed, casts its reflection on the waters of Oxbow Bend and from the edge of Jenny Lake below, Mount St. John rises 11,430 feet.*

Beyond the Colter Bay Marina above left and the banks of Snake River above the Grand Tetons rise abruptly, while at their feet the river meanders slowly back and forth forming the oxbows below which have given their name to Oxbow Bend right and below left. In Bridger Wilderness snow-capped Flat Top Mountain center left forms a dramatic background for Lower Green Lake.

Colter Bay also includes the first trailer park ever added to a National Park. For less than $10, 112 trailers can hook up to water, sewer and electrical connections for the night.

The site of Jackson Lake Lodge was selected personally by Rockefeller. Before he allowed construction to start, he had a scaffolding built to the exact level of the lounge floor so he could see for himself that the view of Jackson Lake and the Tetons would be nothing less than perfect.

It was well worth the trouble. The window in the main lounge is 60-feet wide and two storys high, and the view from it is like nothing else in the world. Rooms in the main lodge range from $40 to $60, as do the rooms in the motor lodge that surrounds it. The difference in price is determined by the view, but there's no such thing as a bad view in Grand Tetons National Park.

The third Rockefeller-built resort, Jenny Lake Lodge, is on an alpine meadow surrounded by quiet forests and bubbling trout streams. The log cabins, some of which have fireplaces, rent for about $130 for two persons to $275 for four. What you get for your money at Jenny Lake is privacy, peace and plenty of quiet.

All the facilities are run on a non-profit basis, and some of the overflow from them is absorbed by stockmen who sold their ranches to make way for the park then leased them back to open dude ranches. And people who once not so lovingly called Rockefeller's Snake River Company "The Snakes", run thriving motels and restaurants today. And the town of Jackson, five miles south of the park, is one of the liveliest towns in Wyoming. In fact, people who live in Teton County are proud to tell you that you haven't lived if you've never been to Jackson on a Saturday night.

The towns that surround both Yellowstone and Grand Teton almost all make the same claim. Typical of them is West Yellowstone, Montana, the western gateway to the park. About 700 people actually live there, but during the "season", which begins on the first weekend in June and continues through Labor Day in September, most of the 2,500,000 people who visit Yellowstone also visit there. That's more people than live in all of Kansas or Oregon and five times as many as live in Atlanta. The town of West Yellowstone is exactly 24 blocks wide, about 640 acres. The president of the Chamber of Commerce unabashedly admits, "It's safe to say this town exists for tourists." It's just as safe to say the man is being modest.

Among the members of the West Yellowstone Chamber of Commerce are about 80 motel owners, some 30 restaurateurs, owners of 50 gift shops, almost 20 gas station operators and a dozen people who run trailer parks.

The police chief and his deputy both run motels, and that's just fine with everybody in town. They agreed long ago to take it easy on people passing through. The town doesn't have a traffic light and stop signs are rare. Parking meters don't exist there, either, because as one local booster put it, "you can't make money from a moving car." The town government doesn't get any income from stopped cars, though. There's no such thing as a parking ticket in West Yellowstone.

Some years ago, the town decided to give people a reason to think of it as a destination rather than a stopping-off place on the way into Yellowstone. They built a theater for summer stock, made square dancing a nightly ritual and began putting on buffalo barbecues as a regular attraction. They converted an old railroad dining hall into a convention center. It's so big that the inside of the fireplace can be used as a stage. And speaking of big…West Yellowstone boasts "the largest natural indoor skating rink west of the Mississippi." It also has an Indian and Animal Museum, and everybody in town is primed to make visitors feel welcome.

But at the converted railroad car that serves as an information center, the most often-asked question is still "Where can I go to see the bears?"

Of all the marvellous things there are to see and do in Yellowstone, seeing the bears is far and away the most popular. The enthusiasm began to build back in the 1920's when a big black bear decided to take a nap in the middle of one of the roads through the park. In the middle of his nap, a tourist bus came along and no amount of horn-blowing could make him get up and move on. One of the passengers, whose experience with animals was obviously limited to zoos, though not to the signs that say "don't feed the animals," tossed a ham sandwich out of the window. The bear gulped it down and let the bus pass. The next day, the same bear was in the same place. He must have had a bus schedule tacked to the wall of his den because, sure enough, along came the bus and from it came another tasty snack.

After several days of playing the game, the bus driver began calling the bear "Jesse James," and it became one of the attraction of the tour to be "held up by Jesse James." As fast as word spread among the tourists, it spread to other bears as well and the begging bears of Yellowstone became as famous as Old Faithful, and a much bigger lure for visitors.

There's a good reason for it. Bears are fun to watch. They're playful and cuddly-cute. In Yellowstone, it's easy to forget they're wild animals with lightning-fast reflexes and enough strength to easily remove the hand that tries to feed them. In spite of strong warnings and strictly-enforced laws against feeding them or treating them as pets, every year dozens of stupid people find out the hard way that these friendly-looking animals can be very dangerous indeed.

The bears who beg along Yellowstone's roads have cultivated a shaggy, bedraggled look. And when they sit up on their hind legs, they do their best to convince you they're starving to death. Only their huge stomachs give the game away. They make a lot of people think of Smokey Bear, a harmless, friendly old character if there ever was one. A few summers ago, a tourist decided it would be fun to take a picture of one of them wearing a ranger hat. He not only didn't get the picture, but lost his camera and it took 20 stitches to close the wound in his hand.

In the West Thumb Geyser Basin of Yellowstone National Park, a brilliant deep blue spring surfaces in Abyss Pool right.

Possibly the dumbest incident on record is the story told by a park ranger who found a man trying to push a bear into the front seat of his car to get a picture of the beast behind the wheel.

No matter how much a bear gets to eat, it is always hungry and the smell of food brings out the beast in them. They've been known to steal locked metal chests and open them for the food inside. They get into the trunks of unlocked cars by tearing out the back seats. And once a bear tore off the front door of a locked car to get a good-smelling picnic lunch from the front seat.

Though all bears are dangerous, that one was obviously more aggressive than others. Years ago, such animals were simply shot to protect the less-intelligent tourists. Today they are captured in a special cage-like trap and taken 30 or 40 miles into the wilderness where tourists rarely go. The animal is marked with a stripe of paint to identify it if it should wander back to its old hunting grounds. If it does, it's given a second chance and another paint stripe. If it should make a third trip back, which rarely happens, the animal is quietly destroyed.

Most of the Yellowstone bears are black bears, but the name refers to the species, not the color. They can be cinnamon, brown or black, and it isn't unusual to see a sow with cubs in each of the three colors. Males and females look alike, about five-feet tall, weighing about 300 pounds. Their cousins, the grizzlies, are much bigger and take life much more seriously. There are some 200 grizzlies in Yellowstone, but you have to take the Park Service's word for it because park visitors rarely see them.

A grizzly bear is probably one of the fiercest animals on earth. Often reaching as much as a half-ton in weight, they can move fast enough to outrun a horse if they don't have to run too far. A century ago, hunters in the Rocky Mountains often reported being attacked by them, but of course, they weren't powerful enough to resist a gun. According to one theory, the memory of their ancestors' violent, sudden deaths encourage today's grizzlies to carefully avoid human contact. Whatever the reason, grizzlies are as stand-offish as black bears are irrepressible.

About the end of October each year the bears get sleepy and look for a cozy cave or hollow log to doze away the winter. Until about a dozen years ago, all Yellowstone, and Grand Teton as well, did pretty much the same thing and the only people who visited the parks were hardy naturalists interested in finding out how bears really do spend the winter or why bull elk leave the cows to themselves after spending the fall months in spectacular fights to build harems. One of the things that kept people away is the 150 or more inches of snow that covers the parks in the winter ("but it's unusual to get more than 18 inches at any one time," says one local enthusiast). Another is the temperature. Back in '33, the West Yellowstone Station reported a drop to 66 below zero. The average in

A welcome fire burning in a landscape blanketed with snow brings unique charm to a campsite at West Thumb right.

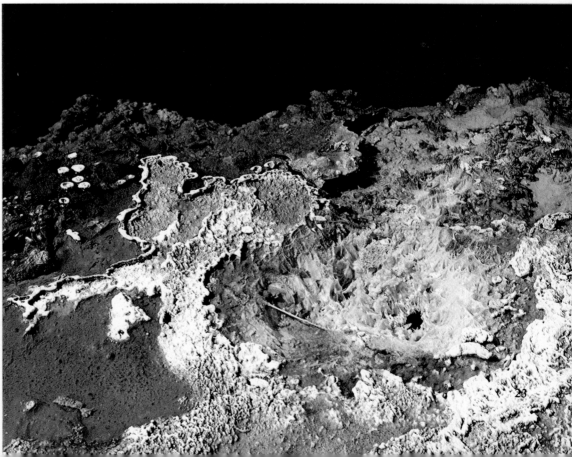

West Thumb Geyser Basin on the shores of Yellowstone Lake left and above is a small, concentrated thermal area of lake shore geysers and hot springs. Among its most spectacular natural features are the Percolating Springs above right, Black Pool below right and Seismograph Pool below.

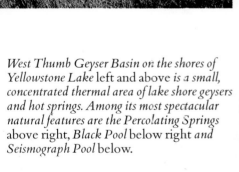

January is just about zero, but the mercury has been known to climb all the way to 35 at that time of year. It must have been one of those days that the idea of a winter season was born. Thousands have bought the idea, and thousands more arrive each winter for a look at the place that more than any other deserves to be called a "winter wonderland."

Big, ten-passenger snowmobiles haul passengers from the West Yellowstone and Mammoth gates to the Snow Lodge in the Old Faithful area. The cost of the adventure is under $20. From the Lodge, the same vehicles, called "snowcoaches", take travelers up to Yellowstone's Grand Canyon for a picnic and a chance to take pictures of the ice-covered canyon and falls. More adventuresome visitors can rent their own snowmobiles for a trip along the Grand Loop Road. All unplowed roads are open for snowmobileing, but to explore the trails, you need snowshoes or cross-country skis. Special marked trails, from three to 20 miles long, are arranged to help the novice or challenge the most experienced. Some have campsites, and all have exciting winter scenery.

At Grand Teton, downhill and cross-country skiing are both big attractions. So is ice fishing on Leigh, Jackson and Jenny Lakes. But the biggest attraction of all is the National Elk Refuge just north of Jackson. Every winter, more than 7,000 elk, the biggest herd in the United States, are on the range there. Visitors get close to them in horse-drawn sleighs they board at Refuge headquarters near Nowlin Creek.

Jackson Hole is also a winter feeding ground for moose, and there's no better time or place for a close-up look at them than the cold months in the valley's willow marshes.

Snow makes animals easier to spot; the winter light makes it easier to watch or photograph them. The winter sun adds a special bonus, too. Low in the sky, it lights up the mountain peaks with dazzling colors the naturalists call "alpenglow." Most of us call it gorgeous.

Naturalists often speak of a "meaningful wilderness experience," and there's no place on earth better to find out what they mean than Yellowstone in winter. Mercifully, the snowmobiles with their irritating "put-put" engines are restricted to the unplowed roads, so it's easily possible to get away from their noise and every other trace of civilization. You can spend hours watching a buffalo digging away the snow to get at the grass under it; or picking up easy-to-follow tracks of a bighorn sheep or antelope, then following them and often finding the animal that made them.

The trees are bent over with snow and the deep snow at your feet cushions every sound. It's a feeling of peace few people are ever lucky enough to experience. And just when you think you've found perfection, Yellowstone gives you something more. The park's geysers and hot springs are at their most fantastic in winter. Rivers and streams flow

Even in June snow lies deep in the mountain forests of Yellowstone National Park left.

Water from rain and snow seeps down through the ground, is heated either by the primal magma of the earth or by underground lava, then surfaces in the form of a geyser or as above and left in the form of a hot spring.

A boardwalk below provides an ideal vantage point from which to view the hydrothermal features of West Thumb Geyser Basin, which seem even more magical in winter right when the steam from hot springs meets the frigid air.

unfrozen through huge snowdrifts, sending up gentle puffs of steam as if to help you find them. Hot springs bubble out over rocks and keep their little territory free of snow all winter long. And when the geysers erupt, the steam is condensed by the cold air and forced to rise higher than it does in the summer. At the top of the column, it billows out into a great mushroom cloud. But the spectacle doesn't end there. When the cloud cools, it drops moisture on the trees and shrubbery. Then the sun catches the ice it makes, and …well, it's the kind of beauty that makes men weep.

Who were the first men to see this fantastic place? They were Indians, of course. Many different tribes lived in or near the area, but the Shoshone were the ones who made a permanent settlement there. They were close relatives of the Comanche, who went down from the mountains to find horses and a new life on the Great Plains. Through the Comanche, the Shoshone got horses, too, and that gave them a big advantage over their enemies, the Blackfeet. When the Blackfeet got guns from the white man, the advantage shifted again and the Shoshone headed for the hills. One branch of the tribe, the Tukarikas, known as Sheep Eaters, were there when hunters, trappers and explorers began arriving in about 1800.

When the Lewis and Clark expedition pushed west in 1805, they passed within about 150 miles from the present site of Yellowstone. On the way back, they crossed the Yellowstone River about 60 miles north of it. It was clear they had heard of the wonders of Yellowstone. In fact, one of their men, John Colter, detached himself from the expedition on the way back to spend the next four years exploring the Rocky Mountains.

When he finally got back to St. Louis and described what he had seen, not many people believed him. And who could blame them? Trappers who had been near the Yellowstone area believed him, though. And to them, the place was known as "Colter's Hell".

Even today a lot of scholars don't believe Colter actually saw the territory that became Yellowstone Park. Even though the National Park Service Museum at Moose in Jackson Hole has a rock inscribed, "John Colter-1808", found in Idaho within sight of the Grand Tetons, they still stick to their guns.

The stone, they say, could be a fraud. And as for Colter's vision of hell; that, they say, was really a description of geothermal activity that occurred in those days along the Shoshone River near Cody, Wyoming. Much of their argument is based on the fact that Colter's wanderings were included in a map published by William Clark to show where he and Meriwether Lewis had gone. He got his information from Colter three years after he had come down out of the mountains, and not only was it done from memory, but Colter died before the map was actually drawn.

In the Upper Geyser Basin steam rises from the aptly named Spasmodic Geyser left.

29

Old Faithful Geyser on these pages *is one of nature's most magnificent spectacles. Although it is not the largest, the highest or the most regular geyser in Yellowstone, it is appropriately named, for since its discovery in 1870 it has remained remarkably consistent. Unlike most thermal features in the Park, its heights, intervals and length of play have changed little in over a century.*

Colter, it should be mentioned, died a natural death on a farm near St. Louis, though he came close to violent death many times during his mountain sojourn.

He hadn't been exploring long when he joined a party headed by Manuel Lisa who had a fort and trading post near the spot where the Yellowstone and Big Horn Rivers come together. Colter's assignment was a tough one. He was told to go find some Indians and convince them they ought to be customers of the trading post. That was what took him into remote territory, and why it's probably true he was among the first white men to have explored the Tetons and Yellowstone.

One of his biographers described the adventure, "...this man, with a pack of thirty pound weight, his gun and some ammunition, went upward of five hundred miles to the Crow nation, gave them information, and proceeded thence to several other tribes."

It wasn't even that simple, of course. At one point, while he was on his way to drum up business at Pierre's Hole, just west of Teton Pass, the party of Crows he was traveling with was attacked by Blackfeet. The Crows were good prospects as customers, so Colter helped them out. In the process, he was wounded in the leg, but helped save his companions from defeat. That didn't sit too well with the Blackfeet who felt humiliated to have been beaten by a paleface. That, combined with his wound, made Colter anxious to get back to Lisa's Fort. He headed north alone, and, according to the story, went directly across the territory that is Yellowstone Park today.

It is a fact that he made it back to the fort safely. And it's also a fact that Lisa gave him a new job. Instead of scouting for business, he was sent out to trap beaver.

One morning when he and a companion were out in their canoes setting traps, they heard rustling noises along the river bank. Convincing each other that it was a herd of buffalo down for a drink, they pressed on.

They were sorry they did when a party of about three hundred Blackfeet appeared on the shore. There was no way to escape, so the white men did what they thought was expected of them when the chiefs motioned them ashore. As Colter's companion's canoe touched the bank, one of the Indians reached out and took his gun. Colter rushed over, grabbed the gun back and gave it to the other white man who, apparently confused, pushed his canoe back into the river. He got an Indian arrow in his leg for that.

Realizing that his wound completely eliminated any thought of escape, he picked up his gun and killed one of the Indians. Their response was to riddle his body with bullets.

That left Colter alone in the hands of a lot of very angry Blackfeet. They were especially irritated about the fact that the white man had died quickly. That was no fun at all for these people who were very inventive about

Tinted by the rays of a setting sun left, *Old Faithful erupts, sending 4,000 to 8,000 gallons of water high into the air.*

making the death of their enemies very slow and very painful. But the good news for them was that they still had a live enemy to deal with. They held a council to decide what to do with him, and after long deliberation, decided to strip him naked and let him run for his life.

Colter was no cream puff, but the territory the Indians wanted him to run through was strewn with sharp stones and tough underbrush, and the Blackfeet were so sure he wouldn't get far without shoes, they gave him a hundred-yard head-start before they started howling after him. And why not? It was fully five miles to the nearest cover, and they didn't want to tear him to pieces before he'd had a little time to think about it.

He had run about 3 miles when he dared to turn his head to see how near death might be. And, wonder of wonders, only one Indian was anywhere near. Slowing down, he called back over his shoulder to ask the brave to spare him. But the Indian would have none of that. Instead, he lunged at Colter with his spear. Fortunately, the long run had tired him, too, and Colter was able to grab the spear before it hit its mark. The head of the spear broke off in his hands, and Colter used it to kill the Indian.

By now the rest of the band was gaining on him, and they were more furious than ever, having watched one of their brothers die at the hands of a naked white man.

Colter sprinted the rest of the way to a river bank and its protective cover of trees. In the middle of the river, he spotted a beaver lodge. As a trapper, he knew the habits of beavers and was well aware that their lodges were built with no entrances except under water. He also knew there was room enough inside for a man to be quite comfortable if he didn't mind not standing up. Without pausing to think about all that, he jumped into the river, quickly found the entrance, and was sitting high and dry inside when the Indians arrived.

They looked everywhere for him. And even though they, too, must have known the habits of beavers, it never occurred to them that a white man could be that much attuned to nature. Before long, they concluded he was still running, and took off in the most likely direction.

Colter stayed put, and it was lucky he did, because a couple of hours later, the Blackfeet came back and poked around some more. They left quickly, muttering to themselves, and by the time the sun went down, Colter figured it was safe enough to come out of hiding.

He was far from safe, of course, and he knew it. Armed with just the broken spearhead, he began a long trek across the mountains. Fearful of Indians, he opted for the tough route, straight up and over the mountains. It took him more than ten days to make it back to the fort.

Later when he told the tale, he said he was no worse for the adventure than the discomfort of "sunburn and sore feet", which is probably one reason why so many people found his tales hard to believe. But the people who welcomed him back to the fort believed every word of this particular story. He was in such bad shape, none of them even recognized him.

An ordinary man would have gone back to civilization at that point. But Colter had a line of traps to tend. On the theory that the Blackfeet would have left the mountains for the winter, he waited until after the first snow to go out to retrieve his pelts. His theory was wrong. He was attacked on the western side of the Continental Divide, narrowly escaped, and was forced to recross the mountains the hard way again.

The following spring, he went back to St. Louis.

Though not many people believed Colter's stories, everyone loved to listen to them, and tales told by other trappers and explorers, as well as the journals of Lewis and Clark, all combined to make the mountain country of the West very attractive indeed. One of the men who was turned on by the tales was John Jacob Astor, who had built a huge fortune on beaver pelts from the wilds of upstate New York.

In 1810, he founded the Pacific Fur Company, then dispatched two expeditions to meet at the mouth of the Columbia River in Oregon to establish a trading village he modestly called "Astoria". The first sailed out of New York

A torrent of water courses its way down densely forested slopes to form the Kepler Cascades above left and right while overleaf the cone of Castle Geyser rises in distinctive silhouette against the evening sky.

34

in a ship which took them around Cape Horn and up the West Coast to the Columbia. For all their trouble, most of the crew was massacred by Indians, who also blew up their ship. But not before they had established Astoria, which was the destination of the overland expedition, which entered Wyoming in midsummer, 1811. They left by way of the Teton Pass.

The Astor expedition, led by Wilson Price Hunt, was the first to cross America after Lewis and Clark, and set out to follow the same route. But after talking with Colter and others, Hunt decided to take a detour south around Blackfoot country, and in the process made the whole country aware of the wonders to be found in northwestern Wyoming.

They blazed a new trail across the country in 340 days. People who worked for Astor generally used the same route taking messages and money back to him. But, on the advice of the Indians, they used a mountain pass somewhat south of the Tetons. In the years that followed, the route, called the Oregon Trail, took thousands to the West looking for a better life. Today it's a highway, Interstate 80, and it still takes thousands across the country. People looking for a beautiful experience turn north from it to head for the Tetons and Yellowstone.

A great many men thought Astor was crazy, not seeing the advantage of trapping in Wyoming. One of them was General William H. Ashley, who started the rush by running ads in eastern newspapers looking for young men who would go into the mountains and bring back furs. The response was overwhelming, and in 1823 men like Jim Bridger, Tom Fitzpatrick and Jim Clyman began wandering through the mountains of Colorado and then north into Wyoming.

It was only a matter of time before they went into business for themselves. Eventually Ashley sold his business to three of his most enterprising employees, Jed Smith, Bill Sublette and Dave Jackson. Smith went west into California and became the first explorer to bring back descriptions of the Sierra Nevada Mountains and the Mojave Desert. Jackson centered his activities in the valley that bears his name, and Sublette went north into the Yellowstone area.

One of the trappers who worked for him, Daniel Potts, wrote a letter in 1826 describing the mud pots and geysers in the West Thumb Basin near Yellowstone Lake. It's the earliest written evidence of white men visiting the area. It was also the first of the millions of letters and postcards that have since recorded first impressions of this unbelievably beautiful spot.

A trapper with the unlikely name of Joe Meek recorded his impressions of the place after having wandered through it in 1829. In a book published 40 years later, Americans were startled to read:

"...The whole country was smoking with vapor from boiling springs and burning with gases issuing from small craters, each of which emitted a sharp whistling sound ...The morning being clear with a sharp frost, Joe thought himself reminded of the city of Pittsburgh, as he had beheld it on a winter morning a couple of years before. ...The general face of the country was smooth and rolling, being a level plain dotted with cone-shaped mounds. On the summit of these mounds were small craters from four to eight feet in diameter. Interspersed among these on the plain were larger craters, some of them from four to six miles across. Out of these craters issued blue flames and molten brimstone."

Mountain men like Joe Meek didn't often leave records of themselves or what they saw. They trekked through the mountains alone or in small groups. Once a year they got together at prearranged rendezvous points where they swapped their furs for clean clothes and fresh whiskey. They swapped yarns, too, and almost everyone had scars and stories from encounters with grizzly bears. Tales of wild Indians abounded, too. But since not many of these people could read or write, their stories went largely unrecorded.

The wife of a missionary who had the misfortune to live near one of their rendezvous points wrote in her diary that she "...could not imagine that white men, brought up in a civilized land, can appear to so much imitate the Devil."

Washington Irving treated them with more Christian charity. "There is perhaps no class of men on the face of the earth." he wrote, "who led a life of more continued exertion, peril and excitement, and who are more enamored of their occupations than the free trappers of the West."

Visitors to the Grand Tetons today find traces of the mountain men at the Park Service Museum at Moose. Even the name of the park itself comes from the name French trappers gave to three of the mountain peaks, Les Trois Tetons. Translated, it means The Three Breasts, which shows where their minds were after months of lugging five-pound traps through knee-deep, icy-cold water.

The trappers usually scheduled their annual rendezvous to coincide with a Fourth of July celebration. Today the celebration is re-enacted on the second Sunday in July at Pinedale, not far south of Jackson. It may be one of the best "Wild West" shows in the country, when hundreds of enthusiastic residents of Sublette County, dressed as trapppers or Indians, gallop into an arena to wait for the big covered wagons, representing the traders out of St. Louis, to roll in. When they do arrive, the jug-toting teamsters, many of whom have been sipping whiskey from the jugs all night long, compete to see who can make their big horses move fastest and stop shortest.

All those still standing at the end of the show are treated to a real western-style barbecue dinner catered by local ranchers. The meal itself is worth the trip.

Many of the trails the mountain men used are marked in both Yellowstone and the Grand Tetons. But their mark on the history of the place was made in just a few short

The gray, rock-like geyserite of Castle Geyser left has been deposited near the mouth and heaped ever higher to produce an imposing cone, with a circumference of 120 feet.

Castle Geyser on these pages *is thought to be the oldest geyser in Yellowstone. Its unusual eruption is in two phases. First it spouts water for thirty minutes, then as here it steams noisily for more than an hour.*

The Morning Glory Pool overleaf *was so named because of the resemblance of its bowl and color to the corolla and color of the beautiful morning glory flower.*

Among Yellowstone's many vividly colored pools, Morning Glory this page and the Emerald Pool in Black Sand Basin overleaf are two of the most remarkable.

years. The last of them drifted away in the early 1840's, calling the area "trapped out".

One of the first to arrive, and last to leave, was Jim Bridger. When the fur business dried up, he went south to build a fort and trading post that became one of the most important stops on the Oregon Trail. At least it was one of the most interesting because Bridger was a wonderful story-teller. And the tales he told were about the wonders to the north.

Bridger knew the Yellowstone area like no other man in the world at that time. But, like Colter before him, his stories were usually considered a pack of lies.

And no wonder! In one of his favorites, he told of the time he spotted a magnificent elk in easy range of his rifle. He took careful aim, he said, and fired at the animal, who not only wasn't hit, but didn't bolt at the sound of the gun. "Maybe he's deaf," thought Jim, and he fired again. Again nothing happened. Four shots later, the elk was still standing there. By then, Bridger was furious. He stormed toward the animal, determined to use his gun as a club. But he ran smack into a wall of glass. Then he discovered the whole mountain was made of glass and inside the elk was still contentedly grazing.

When he collected his wits, he said, he realized that the animal wasn't inside the glass mountain at all, but was 40 miles behind him, reflected in it.

Now, who could believe a story like that?

It's possibly true. There is a glass mountain in Yellowstone Park. It's called Obsidian Cliff. The glass does act as a mirror. The ancient Romans lined their dressing rooms

45

with it for that very reason. The less-vain Indians used it to make arrowheads. The 200-foot glass cliff extends for about a half-mile, changing color in places from jet-black to brown, purple and green with traces of red, yellow and blue. The material, as much real glass as anything any man has ever made, was formed by the quick cooling of molten rock from a volcano.

People today know that Bridger wasn't lying when he said you could catch a trout in Yellowstone Lake and dunk into a boiling pool to cook it without even taking it off the hook. They know he was only stretching the truth a little when he said the fossil forests on Specimen Ridge, with flowers turned into quartz crystals, was the work of an angry Crow medicine man who put a curse on the place.

Western migrants were fascinated by Bridger's yarns, but not enough to keep them from going further west, and the Yellowstone area stayed shrouded in mystery for another 20 years.

Then gold was discovered in Montana. Springtime in the Rockies in 1863 brought thousands to places like the Big Prickly Pear, Pioneer Creek and Alder Gulch. By mid-summer, an expedition was put together to "prospect" the country to the south. In their travels, they went through the Yellowstone Geyser Basins, but they were too busy looking down for traces of gold to know what they had found. Four years earlier, a Government-sponsored scientific expedition had also passed through the territory, but their mission had been to observe a solar eclipse, so they were too busy looking up to notice the wonders around them.

Though none of the prospectors struck it rich, parties of them tramped through the area every summer for several years. Some wrote stories about what they saw for local newspapers, and little by little, people all over the country became aware of this strange, mysterious place.

Finally, in 1869, an expedition was put together to put the wild stories to rest once and for all. Or to prove they were true.

David E. Folsom, C. W. Cook and William Peterson entered the present limits of the Park near today's North Entrance in Montana. In their 36-day trip, they found the falls of the Yellowstone River as well as the spectacular Grand Canyon. They explored Sulphur Mountain and Mud Volcano, and then went down the west shore of Yellowstone Lake with its beautiful springs and over the mountains to Shoshone Lake where they turned north again to head back to Montana. On their way, they explored the Lower Geyser Basin and became the first white men to watch the spectacular Fountain Geyser send its plume 75 feet into the air.

When they got back, they were reluctant to talk much about their trip. According to one report, "they were unwilling to risk their reputations for veracity by a full recital (of the marvels they had seen) to a small company whom their friends had assembled to hear the account of their explorations".

But David Folsom decided to take a chance. He wrote an article about Yellowstone that was published in a Chicago magazine, *Western Monthly,* in 1870. It was a strange tale, but people were ready to believe it, and in the summer of that year, an expedition of nine men went into the area. Included in the party were Henry D. Washburn, Surveyor General of Montana, Nathaniel P. Langford, who would later be the first superintendant of the world's first national park, and Lieutenant Gustavus C. Doan of the Second Cavalry in command of a four-man military escort.

They were willing to believe Folsom's story, but one of them later wrote, "I think a more confirmed set of sceptics never went out into the wilderness than those who composed our party, and never was a party more completely surprised and captivated with the wonders of nature".

The first wonder they saw was Devil's Slide and the mountain they called Cinnabar because they thought the bright red stone was cinnabar ore. But they hadn't seen anything yet! They were still outside the present boundaries of the park.

They were so impressed by Tower Falls, they spent two days admiring the 132-foot cataract and the wonderful rock formations around it. Even the military man, Doan, had to say, "nothing can be more chastely beautiful than this lovely cascade, hidden away in the dim light of overshadowing rocks and woods, its very voice hushed to a low murmur, unheard at a distance of a few hundred yards".

Like Adam and Eve in the Garden of Eden, the expedition flitted from place to place giving names to everything they saw. They came up with the name Tower Creek because its canyon looked like "some old castle". Obviously inspired by tales of Colter's Hell, they named one of the more spectacular pinnacles Devil's Hoof and a whole group of towers above the falls Devil's Den. They found the Washburn Hot Springs, later named for the leader of the expedition, and called them "Hell Broth Springs".

They explored and described the spectacular Grand Canyon of the Yellowstone. But a few days before they had found another canyon downstream that had taken their breath away. Doane wrote in his diary, "standing on the brink of the chasm the heavy roaring of the imprisoned river comes to the ear in a sort of hollow, hungry growl, scarcely audible from the depths and strongly suggestive of demons in torment below. (It is) grand, gloomy and terrible, an empire of shadows and turmoil".

They got a good look at the empire that would become Yellowstone Park in exactly the same way visitors to the park do today, by climbing to the top of the 10,317-foot Mount Washburn. Today you can get there by bus, but in 1870 it was a long walk, and Washburn himself begged off when his companions went up to have a look around.

What they saw was Yellowstone Lake, with the river flowing north from it, and, of course, the Grand Canyon, stretching 24 miles into the distance. Though they named

The stark, twisted outlines of dead trees rise from the floor of Black Sand Basin right *and Opalescent Pool overleaf.*

The Upper Geyser Basin Trail below *leads through a mysterious landscape of magnificent shapes and colors. Opalescent Pool* left *brings reflections in ever changing shades to Black Sand Basin and the area around Grotto Geyser* below right *is touched with a distinctive red. Geyserite deposited on trees which once grew around the geyser has contributed to the extraordinary shape of Grotto Geyser itself* above.

Grand Geyser above right *is the largest predictable geyser now active. Unlike most geysers, its orifice is at the bottom of a pool some 25 feet deep. More erratic are the geysers in the Daisy Geyser Group* center right *which are capable of erupting quite unexpectedly.*

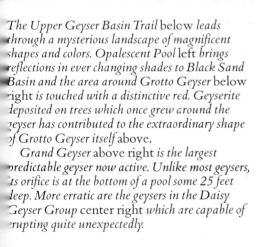

nearly everything else, the Yellowstone River already had a name. The Indians called it that, and now the explorers had a good idea why as they admired the beautiful coloring of the canyon walls. Had they been there in the spring when the snow was melting or after a heavy summer rain, they would have seen the brilliant yellow and red color of the stone at its very best. But even in the dry season the canyon was so beautiful that one of them said he "stayed two hours in one spot and drank in inspiration".

The party stayed in the canyon for more than a day admiring the falls and congratulating themselves on being the first men to walk on the floor of the canyon.

A few days later, after exploring the area around Mud Volcano, which they said made noises like "the bursting of heavy guns," then scaling (and naming) Mount Doane and Mount Langford, they began to travel around Yellowstone Lake. It was there that disaster struck. Truman Everts got separated from the party, and after a few days of searching, was given up for dead. The expedition pressed on, delayed by an 18-inch snowfall (on September 15!), and wanting nothing more than to get back to Helena and their warm beds.

It was cold, their feet were wet, their horses dragging. They were depressed about the fate of poor Everts and even the quiet beauty of the thick pine forest seemed more oppressive than inspiring.

Then, all of a sudden, they came upon a wonder the like of which none of them had yet seen. Ahead of them in an open valley, a jet of steam and water was rising at least a hundred and fifty feet into the air and the steam was caught in the breeze that spread it like a huge curtain across the valley floor.

"We spurred our jaded horses," said one, "to gather around this wonderful phenomenon." It didn't take them long to give the phenomenon a name. They stayed in the area for a day, and noticed they could almost set their watches by this beautiful geyser. And so they named it Old Faithful.

You can't exactly set your watch by it, but Old Faithful erupts on average every 66 minutes. Each eruption lasts about four minutes, during which time it sends about 10,000 gallons of scalding water 150 feet into the air. Amateur photographers should note that the best part of the show is at the end and not the beginning, and it's best to stand far enough back to get the whole column into the picture. No two eruptions are the same, either, so stick around, you'll get a different shot next time.

The Washburn party discovered seven geysers before they left the Upper Geyser Basin, including the one they named The Giant, the highest geyser in the world. It's less popular than Old Faithful, even though it erupts as much as 250 feet, and continues as long as an hour and a half. It's not as reliable, erupting only every six to 15 days. They named The Giantess Geyser, too, and she gushes almost 200 feet when she feels like it, which is rarely.

Just north of Castle Geyser lies Crested Pool left, *the depths of which are a magnificent intense blue.*

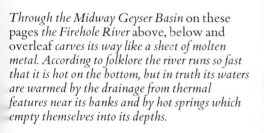

Through the Midway Geyser Basin on these pages *the Firehole River* above, below and overleaf *carves its way like a sheet of molten metal. According to folklore the river runs so fast that it is hot on the bottom, but in truth its waters are warmed by the drainage from thermal features near its banks and by hot springs which empty themselves into its depths.*

There are 142 geysers in the Basin ranging from the Anemone that spits a few feet into the air for 30 seconds, to the Catfish that rises almost 8 feet almost all the time.

It's also the location of the present-day Old Faithful Inn, a rustic hotel with prices ranging from about $40 for a deluxe double room to about $20 for less elegant accommodations. All the rooms have space for more than two persons, and additional sleepers pay less than $4 each to double up.

The Inn is open from early May through mid-September. The nearby Lodge and Cabins have a shorter season, but also feature shelters that can accommodate up to four people for less than $12.

The shelters have electric heat and hot and cold running water. If they had been there in 1870, the Washburn party might not have pushed on for home as quickly as they did.

But they got back to Montana before the winter set in and spent the cold months telling the world what they saw. For the first time, the world believed it.

Lieutenant Doane's official report went to Washington by February, and by spring others in the party had articles published in national magazines. Meanwhile, the lost Truman Everts had found his way back to civilization in October after more than a month of wandering, and romanticized tales of his survival made Yellowstone that much more fascinating.

It isn't easy even now to find your way through the thick woodlands of Yellowstone should you wander off the trail. It was doubly tough for the 54-year-old Everts who was nearsighted, and had broken his glasses. If he wanted to examine a trail, he had to get down on his knees to do it. Fortunately, he did have a small pair of binoculars which helped him see and also helped him build fires when the sun was out. But he didn't have a gun to provide food, and to add to his bad luck, his horse wandered off on the second day of his ordeal.

After his rescue, he moved back east to New York, where he died 30 years later. No one missed him in Montana. When he wasn't wandering in the woods, he was collector of internal revenue for the territory.

The stories inspired a more ambitious exploration the following summer when the Government, as if to confirm them, dispatched two expeditions, one led by Dr. Ferdinand Hayden, a geologist, the other a military group co-commanded by Colonel John W. Barlow and Captain David P. Heap. It was a classis case of government overkill.

Though they covered much of the same ground as the 1870 expedition, they explored the Mammoth Hot Springs area, which Hayden called White Mountain Hot Springs but Barlow insisted ought to be called Soda Mountain. They also wandered through Specimen Ridge before heading south for the Grand Canyon and a look at the falls.

Although the seriousness of the enterprise was in doubt because the military men were said to be fond of two-hour lunches and Barlow carried an umbrella to protect him from the sun and the best anyone could say about Heap was that he was "a small man", both parties had photographers with them. And for insurance, the Army took along an artist to sketch what they saw.

In addition to their photographs and sketches, they made five maps between them, and though none was accurate, they added to the picture. It was a picture it didn't take Washington long to understand.

Within five months of the end of the twin expeditions, on March 1, 1872, President Grant signed the bill that made Yellowstone America's first National Park. The idea had been first proposed over a campfire near the spot where the Gibbon and Firehole Rivers come together. On the night of September 19, 1870, members of the Washburn party fell to discussing what God had created there and what would happen when man would come along to improve it.

Some of them mentioned it would be a good idea to claim the land around some of the natural wonders "for speculation." But a cooler head, Cornelius Hedges, had a better idea. Private ownership would ruin the place, he reasoned, and the whole territory ought to be retained by the government for unrestricted use of the people.

It was a convincing argument, and he pushed it forward later in the year in an article he published in the Helena Herald. Meanwhile, Nathaniel P. Langford, another member of the party, went on a lecture tour that took him to Washington, Chicago and New York. His message was picked up in an editorial in The New York Herald Tribune which said, ". . . this new field of wonders should be at once withdrawn from occupancy and set apart as a public national park for the enjoyment of the American people for all time."

In the Midway Geyser Basin, steaming water above *cascades into the Firehole River, which wends its way more peacefully through the Upper Geyser Basin* overleaf.

The Great Fountain Geyser above left *erupts with powerful bursts which can reach almost 200 feet above its tremendous terraces, while nearby* White Dome Geyser right, *with its beautiful 12 foot cone, spurts steam from an orifice only 4 inches wide.*

Spasm Geyser below *is one of the spectacular features on the Fountain Paint Pot Nature Trail.*

61

The boardwalk of the Midway Geyser Basin skirts the very edge of Yellowstone's largest hot spring, Grand Prismatic Spring on these pages. A blue haze rises above the water and rings of orange and yellow algae and bacteria form a huge prism around the deep blue of the pool which is 370 feet in diameter.

Mud springs caused by the action of fumaroles leading to a basin below the water table produce the Fountain Paint Pots overleaf.

Back in Montana, the expedition veterans went to work on the political front and convinced their Territorial Congressional Delegate, William H. Clagett, to formalize their dream with a bill in Congress. Then the blitz began. They went to Washington at every opportunity, and made sure that every member of Congress got copies of every magazine and newspaper article written about the Yellowstone area.

The bill was introduced on December 18, 1871 and signed into law the following March, an incredibly short space of time. And it was an incredible idea. Throughout history, it wasn't unusual for tracts of forests, islands, mountain tops to be set aside as retreats for royalty or privileged classes. But until Yellowstone, no one ever thought of reserving such a huge tract of land for the enjoyment of all the people. A British Earl who toured the park two years later said, "... It was an act worthy of a great nation, and she will have her reward in the praise of the present army of tourists, no less than in the thanks of the generations of them yet to come."

Yellowstone is still the biggest National Park in the world, covering more than two *million* acres, and National Forests around it cover eight *million* more. More people than live in the three states that contain it visit Yellowstone each year. And, by the way, it was a park before any of them were states.

The Indians thought it was the top of the world, and for them it was. Rivers flow in every direction from it, and it's possible to cross and recross the Continental Divide more than once without leaving the same road.

Except for the bears, Yellowstone is possibly best-known for its geysers and other "thermal features." The Park Service estimates there are more than ten thousand of them. No wonder they called it "Colter's Hell."

The statistics are amazing. There are 165 streams, each containing an uncounted number of trout, most with waterfalls and cataracts that invite you to stop and have a look. There are 36 lakes, covering a total area of 165 square miles. There are valleys and canyons, mountain peaks and hillsides. And all the stones aren't yellow, They come in every amazing color nature can provide. And, yes, if the prospectors had only kept at it, some of it is gold and silver up near Crescent Hill Canyon.

The animal population is incredible, ranging from meadow mice to moose. There are herds of buffalo, bands of bighorn sheep, packs of coyotes. In the fall, eagles come north to feed on salmon, who make the same trip the hard way. They often compete with ospreys for the same morsels, and the thousands of ducks carefully stay out of the way of both. There are swans and cranes, even pelicans, on the lakes. There are hawks and meadowlarks, hummingbirds and herons and, forever changing the landscape, incredibly busy beavers. Some years ago, they cut down all the trees in a valley near Obsidian Cliff and

At the Falls of the Gibbon left *the river tumbles 84 feet in a thin white veil.*

69

Yellowstone is America's largest wildlife preserve and its dramatic countryside is the refuge of a wide variety of species, among them the pronghorn (antelope) below, deer above, wapiti (elk) above and center right and the moose left, the largest member of the park's deer family. It is the bison however, center and below right and bottom, which reigns supreme as Yellowstone's largest animal. Weighing up to 2,000 pounds, he is nevertheless capable of galloping up to 40 mph. Part of the natural beauty which makes this so idyllic a preserve, the Gibbon River overleaf threads its silver waters between imposing pines.

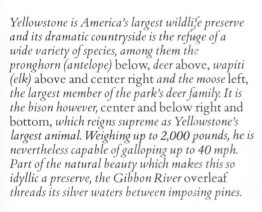

In the Hayden Valley left the Yellowstone River spreads into broad, curving channels and wildlife including herds of elk right and bison below abounds. Lodgepole pines above left and woodlands near Bridge Bay above provide welcome protective cover from the heat of the sun and human intrusion.

Beyond Hayden Valley the river picks up speed and carves its way ever deeper into the magnificent Grand Canyon of the Yellowstone overleaf.

75

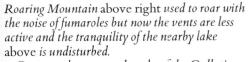

Roaring Mountain *above right used to roar with the noise of fumaroles but now the vents are less active and the tranquility of the nearby lake* above *is undisturbed.*

Between the crags and peaks of the Gallatin Mountains, the Gallatin River *center right and* below *flows through its valley.*

To many the Norris Geyser Basin *with* Nuphar Lake *left and* Crackline Lake *right is the most fascinating thermal area in the park.* Porcelain Basin *overleaf which forms the northern half of it derives its name from the gray-white geyserite which covers most of the cup in which the thermal features are located.*

used the sticks to turn the valley into a pond. Then, as if looking for something to keep themselves occupied, they cut a hole in the dam to let the water out. Since the pond was quite beautiful, park engineers repaired the damage. They had no sooner packed up their gear when the animals cut another hole. After three tries, the engineers gave up.

Ecologically, Yellowstone is divided into five distinct

Above: *Echinus Geyser.*   Top: *Cistern Spring.*

Right: *Steamboat Geyser, the most powerful in Yellowstone, shoots its water 300-350 feet into the sky.*

zones that range from alpine conditions, with plant life usually found only in the arctic, to lush grassy valleys thousands of feet closer to sea level. Visitors find it easier to explore by thinking of it as five separate parks. The Old Faithful area, with its Inn, lodges and cabins, is probably the place most people begin.

Yellowstone Lake has a fine hotel, too, with about the same low rates as in the Old Faithful area. Not far away, at Fishing Bridge, there are 350 paved sites for overnight parking of recreational vehicles at a cost of well under $10. Cabins in the area rent for under $35 for two people with a small additional fee for up to four persons more.

You can rent boats there, hire a fishing guide or take a bus tour along the beautiful lake shore. For about $4, you can take an excursion boat out into the lake for a peek at the islands, an experience most visitors missed in the early days of the park.

There are overnight facilities at Canyon Village, including a public campground. You can also rent a saddle horse there and take a ride with a real Wyoming wrangler.

A little to the north, near Tower Falls, Roosevelt Lodge offers a genuine Old West experience including stagecoach rides and dinner cooked outdoors from the back of a chuckwagon. Six people can rent a cabin there for under $15.

The accommodations are a bit more expensive (but not much more!) at Mammoth Hot Springs, where six people can rent a cabin for under $30. It's located near the original park entrance and the park's headquarters. The hot springs there are unusual even for Yellowstone. They rise in terraces and have formed overhanging bowls with fantastic colors. The water is transparent and takes on the color of the sky, which in that part of the world is a spectacle in itself.

When the park was originally created, there was no such thing as a park ranger and the job of keeping poachers away as well as protecting animals and tourists from each other fell to the military. A fort was built to house the troops in the Mammoth area, and it was the center of their activity until 1918 when park protection became a civilian job.

There was a ranger in Yellowstone long before that, though. Back in 1880, the government hired an old mountain man named Harry Yount to be Yellowstone's gamekeeper. His job was to patrol the park during the snowy months to make sure no other people were there. Harry didn't mind spending the winter alone. In fact, he enjoyed the distinction of being the first to survive a Yellowstone winter. But when he was asked to file an official report in the spring, he pointed out it wasn't possible for one man to patrol all of Yellowstone, even with all that time to do it. He proposed a protective force, and when Congress finally got around to taking his advice nearly 30 years later, old-timers were fond of saying that Harry was the first of the rangers. And a lone ranger at that.

There are thousands of rangers today, keeping order, answering questions, helping people in trouble and generally taking care of the 37 National Parks as well as the 257 other facilities of the system, including national monuments, national seashores, parkways, battlefields and more.

Rangers and other park employees divide visitors into two basic types. In the early days, people who arrived by train or stagecoach were referred to as "dudes." People who

At Mammoth, *Minerva Terrace* previous page, above and below left and right, *New Highland Terrace* below *and White Elephant Back Terrace* above *are beautiful terraces made of travertine, a form of calcium carbonate that has been dissolved from limestone beneath the ground and carried to the surface by hot water. The colors on the terraces are tiny plants, algae and bacteria.*

Heavy with snow the branches of countless fir trees overhang Scaup Lake overleaf.

drove their own cars, and who usually camped out overnight, were called "sagebrushers." These days almost everyone arrives by car, so the criteria have changed. Today's "dudes" are people who stay in park hotels, "sagebrushers" still camp out at night.

The rangers themselves are divided into two groups, the ones they call "90-day wonders" are usually college students and teachers who are added to the force during the busy months. The ones who work all year are called "old timers." In either case, they're men and women who like people as much as they love nature. They have to be part mountaineer, woodsman, geologist, meteorologist, historian, botanist, zoologist, naturalist, teacher, guide and police officer. In recent years, linguistics has been a good qualification to add to their job description. They run the visitor centers and museums. They give lectures and conduct campfire programs. They field questions, thoughtful and otherwise. They even risk their lives to help visitors in danger.

It's best to think of them as your hosts when you visit a national park. It's how they think of themselves.

What lures them to Yellowstone and The Tetons is the same thing that lures the rest of us there. It's what Thoreau was talking about when he said "We need the tonic of wilderness."

The parks are something more than just wilderness. The Algonquins and other Eastern Indian tribes must have had this spot in mind when they told stories of young men searching for God and heaven itself by traveling west and finding both in a mysteriously beautiful mountain. No one can come away from this place without having experienced a deep emotion about it, and very few can find the words to describe how they feel.

It's the feeling you get in the evening after one of those spectacular Western sunsets during the half hour or so of soft light just before the sky begins to sparkle with a billion stars. Standing at the edge of a meadow with its carpet of buttercups, Indian paintbrush and forget-me-nots, you see a family of deer gingerly stepping out of the woods on the way to a laughing stream for a cold drink. In the bushes nearby, sparrows are setting up a racket as if to warn the world that something momentous is about to happen, and in the grass, a bluebird softens the sound. Overhead, a falcon is floating on the wind looking for his last meal of the day. Underfoot, a chipmunk runs for cover to make sure he isn't the meal.

It's moments like that, that makes you wish you could live for ever, times like when you find out what the word "peace" really means.

In the mountains of Northwestern Wyoming, moments like those come often, and the best part is that anyone can experience them. Yellowstone, and The Tetons, too, was created for that simple reason. You'll find it engraved on the gate at Mammoth Hot Springs. The parks are there "For The Benefit And Enjoyment Of The People."

Above right: *Shoshone National Forest.*
Center right: *Lamar River Valley.*
Below right: *Fishing Bridge.*

iewed from Inspiration Point previous page *nd from Grand View Point* left, *the Yellowstone iver is dwarfed by sheer canyon walls of dark va, thickly forested on either side of foaming falls. t the Upper Falls* below right *the torrent arches acefully out and down for 109 feet and at the wer Falls* above, above right, below and *erleaf it thunders down a breathtaking 308 t, spreading foam and mist for a remarkable stance.*

First published 1980 by Colour Library International Ltd.
© 1980 Illustrations and text: Colour Library International Ltd., 163 East 64th St., New York, N.Y.10021.
Colour separations by La Cromolito, Milan, Italy.
Display and text filmsetting by Focus Photoset, England.
Printed and bound by JISA-RIEUSSET, Barcelona, Spain.
ISBN 0-8317 9974-9 Library of Congress Catalogue Card No. 79-90593
Published in the United States of America by Mayflower Books, Inc., New York City.

D.L.B.11966